This book belongs to:

. . . .

. . . .

This is a Parragon Publishing Book
This edition published in 2002

Parragon Publishing
Queen Street House
4 Queen Street
Bath BA1 1HE, UK

This book was created by
small world creations ltd
Tetbury, UK

Written by Janet Allison Brown
Designed by Sarah Lever

Copyright © Parragon 2001

Printed in China

ISBN 0-75257-645-3

Baby Record Book

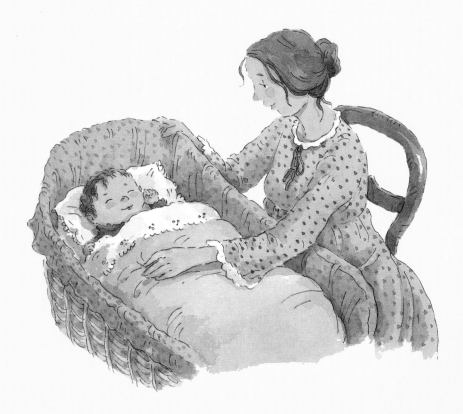

p

What's To Come...

The First Nine Months

It takes nine months to grow a baby—that's a long time
to wait for something really exciting to happen!

Mommy and Daddy first found out I was coming on . . . .

Their first reaction was: (Mommy) . . . .

(Daddy) . . . .

They first heard my heartbeat on . . . .

Mommy first felt me kicking on . . . .

Whilest she was pregnant with me, Mommy had some strange food
cravings. Here are some of them: . . . .

. . . .

Here is a picture of my first sonogram. It doesn't look much like
me—just wait till I start growing!

Photo

This sonogram was taken on . . . .

Ride a Cock-horse

Ride a cock-horse to Banbury Cross
To see a fine lady ride on a white horse
Rings on her fingers and bells on her toes
She shall have music wherever she goes!

Family Tree

Families are like apple trees—they grow branches and yield lots of fruit!
This is the family I was born into.

Father's Parents

Mother's Parents

Parents

Brothers

Baby

Sisters

Mommy's name is

. . . .

She was born on

. . . .

Daddy's name is

. . . .

He was born on

. . . .

Mommy and Daddy first met on

. . . .

Other family members are . . . .

. . . .

. . . .

Mary, Mary, Quite Contrary

Mary, Mary, quite contrary,
How does your garden grow?
With silver bells and cockle shells,
And pretty maids all in a row.

 My Birth

All good things come to those who wait–and at last I arrived, the latest
rosy apple on the family tree!

I was expected on

Day. . . . . Month. . . . . Date. . . . . . . Year. . . . . . .

I arrived on

Day. . . . . Month. . . . . . . Date. . . . . . . Year. . . . . . .

I was born at . . . .

Monday's Child

Monday's child is fair of face,

Tuesday's child is full of grace,

Wednesday's child is full of woe,

Thursday's child has far to go,

Friday's child is loving and giving,

Saturday's child works hard for a living,

But the child that is born on the Sabbath day

Is happy and bright in every way.

These are the people who helped

Mommy at my birth:

. . . .

. . . .

. . . .

. . . .

. . . .

. . . .

Hey Diddle Diddle

Hey diddle diddle, the cat and the fiddle,
The cow jumped over the moon;
The little dog laughed to see such sport,
And the dish ran away with the spoon!

Photo

My Appearance

Newborn babies don't look like anything, except—newborn babies! But after a while they start to resemble other people in the family.

Bye, Baby Bunting

Bye, baby bunting,
Daddy's gone a-hunting!
To fetch a little rabbit skin
To wrap the baby bunting in.

This is how I looked when I was born:

Eyes: . . . .

Hair: . . . .

Weight: . . . .

Length: . . . .

These are the changes in my appearance that took place over the first few weeks of my life:. . . . .

. . . .

. . . .

Mommy says I look like. . . . .

Daddy says I look like. . . . .

Other people say I look like. . . . .

Here's a photograph of me at . . . . weeks old.

I think I look just like me!

Photo

I Am Me

I am me

Who else could I be?

 # First Days

Babies do a lot of sleeping in their first few days, and I was no exception!

These are some of the other things I did:

. . . .

. . . .

. . . .

. . . .

Lots of people were curious to see me. Some of my first visitors

were. . . . .

. . . .

. . . .

. . . .

Rock-a-Bye Baby

Rock-a-bye baby on the treetop,
When the wind blows, the cradle will rock;
When the bough breaks, the cradle will fall,
And down will come baby, cradle and all.

Mommy and I got lots of cards and presents.
Here are a few of them:

. . . . from. . . . .

. . . . from. . . . .

. . . . from. . . . .

. . . . from. . . . .

Hush, Little Baby

Hush, little baby, don't say a word,
Daddy's going to buy you a mocking bird.
If that mocking bird won't sing,
Daddy's going to buy you a diamond ring.
If that diamond ring is brass,
Daddy's going to buy you a looking-glass.
If that looking-glass gets broke,
Daddy's going to buy you a billy goat.
If that billy goat runs away,
Daddy's going to buy you another today.

Coming Home

Home is where the heart is, and I was glad to arrive safely
at my home!

Mommy and Daddy brought me home for the first time on . . . .

. . . .

My new home is at:. . . . .

. . . .

My family has lived here for: . . . .

These are the people who live in my home: . . . .

. . . .

. . . .

These are the people who were waiting to greet me when I first came

home:. . . . .

. . . .

. . . .

. . . .

. . . .

. . . .

On my first night home, I fell asleep

at . . . .

. . . .

and woke up at . . . .

. . . .

East, West

East, west
Home is best.

 # My Name

Some babies are named after their Mommy and Daddy or their grandparents. Others are named after friends. No matter how it happens, a name is for life, so it's important to get it right!

These are some of the names that Mommy and Daddy thought they might give me:

If I were a girl: . . . .

If I were a boy: . . . .

But they decided to name me: . . . .

because: . . . .

My nickname is: . . . .

because: . . . .

My Christening or Naming Day celebration was on: . . . .

at: . . . .

My godparents are: . . . .

. . . .

. . . .

Here's a photograph of me on my special day!

Photo

Elizabeth, Elspeth, Betsy and Bess

Elizabeth, Elspeth, Betsy and Bess,
They all went together to seek a bird's nest
They found a bird's nest with five eggs in
They all took one, and left four in.

The Announcement

Everybody likes to hear that a new baby has arrived safely!

My birth was announced in the following way:. . . . .

. . . .

These are the words Mommy and Daddy used to announce my

arrival: . . . .

. . . .

. . . .

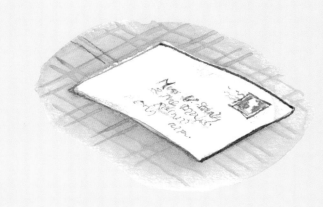

Because I was born in the month of . . . .

my star sign is . . . .

These are some of the characteristics of my star sign:. . . . .

. . . .

. . . .

And here are some of my own early characteristics!. . . . .

. . . .

. . . .

Hark! Hark! The Dogs Do Bark

Hark! Hark! The dogs do bark

Beggars are coming to town

Some in rags

And some in tags

And one in a velvet gown!

Hands, Feet, Hair, Teeth!

Here are outline of my hands and feet that
Mommy and Daddy drew when I
was. . . . . months old!

Here's my hand. . .

. . . here's my foot. . .

. . . . and here's a lock of my hair!

I began teething on . . . .

My first tooth appeared on . . . .

My second tooth appeared on . . . .

My third tooth appeared on . . . .

My forth tooth appeared on . . . .

My fifth tooth appeared on . . . .

I had a full set of teeth on . . . .

Curly Locks, Curly Locks

Curly Locks, Curly Locks, will you be mine?

You shall not wash dishes, nor yet feed the swine

But sit on a cushion and sew a fine seam

And dine upon strawberries, sugar, and cream.

Growth Chart

Like a little seedling, I soon started to sprout upward! This chart shows my progress.

	DATE	HEIGHT	WEIGHT
I am 3 months old:	_____	_____	_____
I am 6 months old:	_____	_____	_____
I am 9 months old:	_____	_____	_____
I am 12 months old:	_____	_____	_____
I am 18 months old:	_____	_____	_____
I am 36 months old:	_____	_____	_____

Here is a photograph to show how much I changed!

Photo

Girls and Boys, Come Out to Play

Girls and boys, come out to play,
The moon does shine as bright as day.
Come with a whoop, and come with a call,
Come with a good will, or not at all!

First Sounds

At first I couldn't say very much, but I liked to say it LOUDLY! Soon I learned which sounds produced food, and which ones made everyone smile.

The first sounds I made were . . . .

The first word I ever said was . . . . on . . . .

I first laughed on . . . .

at (e.g. Mommy/Daddy/a song): . . . .

I first said "Mummy" on . . . .

I first said "Daddy" on . . . .

I spoke my first complete sentence on . . . .

This is what I said . . . .

. . . .

This is how everyone reacted . . . .

. . . .

. . . .

. . . .

One, Two, Buckle My Shoe

One, two, buckle my shoe;
Three, four, open the door;
Five, six, pick up sticks;
Seven, eight, lay them staight;
Nine, ten, start again!

 First Steps

It wasn't long before I discovered that the world was an interesting place,
with lots to see and TOUCH!

I first held my head up on: . . . .

I first clapped my hands on: . . . .

I first rolled all the way over on: . . . .

I first started to crawl on: . . . .

I first sat up on: . . . .

I first started pulling myself to my feet on: . . . .

And I took my first steps on: . . . .

when I was : . . . . months old. I was walking

toward: . . . . and everyone thought I was very clever!

Dr. Foster Went to Gloucester

Dr. Foster went to Gloucester
In a shower of rain;
He stepped in a puddle, right up to his middle,
And never went there again!

Round and Round the Garden

Round and round the garden
Like a teddy bear;
One step, two steps
Tickley under there!

Special "Firsts"

Everything was new and exciting to me. This page is a record of some of the 'firsts' I experienced in the first year of my life.

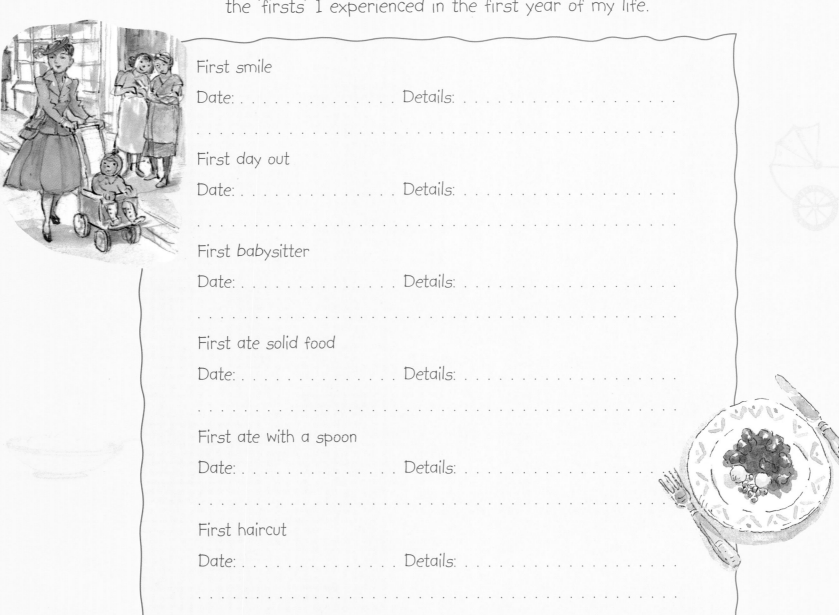

First smile

Date: . . . . Details: . . . .

. . . .

First day out

Date: . . . . Details: . . . .

. . . .

First babysitter

Date: . . . . Details: . . . .

. . . .

First ate solid food

Date: . . . . Details: . . . .

. . . .

First ate with a spoon

Date: . . . . Details: . . . .

. . . .

First haircut

Date: . . . . Details: . . . .

. . . .

First friends

Date: . . . . Details: . . . .

. . . .

First saw snow

Date: . . . . Details: . . . .

. . . .

Other firsts

Date: . . . . Details: . . . .

. . . .

Date: . . . . Details: . . . .

. . . .

Date: . . . . Details: . . . .

. . . .

My Likes and Dislikes

Some things made me laugh! Other things made me cry. These are some of my early likes and dislikes, with special attention to the most important thing of all—FOOD!

I liked . . . .

But I didn't like . . . .

I liked . . . .

But I didn't like . . . .

I liked . . . .

But I didn't like . . . .

I liked . . . .

But I didn't like . . . .

I especially LOVED . . . .

And I especially DIDN'T LIKE . . . .

Jack Sprat

Jack Sprat could eat no fat, his wife could eat no lean;
And so, between the two of them, they licked the platter clean!

Pease Porridge Hot

Pease porridge hot, pease porridge cold
Pease porridge in the pot, nine days old!

Bath and Bedtime

Mommy and Daddy soon discovered that I did/did not like to be bathed.

This is their description of me in the bath:

. . . .

. . . .

I had my first bath at home on:. . . . .

My favorite bath toys are:. . . . .

. . . .

Rub-a-Dub-Dub

Rub-a-dub-dub, three men in a tub
And how do you think they be?
The butcher, the baker, the candlestick-maker
They all jumped out of a rotten potato!
Turn 'em out, knaves all three?

The Man in the Moon

The man in the moon
Looked out of the moon
And this is what he said:
"Now that I'm getting up, 'tis time
All the children went to bed!"

I first slept in a crib on . . . .

My favorite bedtime toys are . . . .

My favorite bedtime teddy is . . . .

My favourite lullabies are . . . .

I first slept through the night on . . . .

Mommy and Daddy were very happy!

Here's a picture of me in pajamas!

Photo

My Health

It's surprising how many injections and tests a poor little baby needs! And how many coughs, colds and sniffles a child can catch. Here is a medical history of my first year.

Injections

Date: My age: Details:

. . . .

Date: My age: Details:

. . . .

Date: My age: Details:

. . . .

Eye tests

Date: My age: Details:

. . . .

Date: My age: Details:

. . . .

Hearing tests

Date: My age: Details:

. . . .

Date: My age: Details:

. . . .

Illnesses

Date: .... My age: .... Details: ....

Date: .... My age: .... Details: ....

Date: .... My age: .... Details: ....

I am allergic to . . . .

. . . .

The doctor who looked after me was . . . .

Early to Bed

Early to bed and early to rise
Makes a man healthy, wealthy, and wise.

My First Christmas

My first Christmas was a special occasion. The house was
decorated with lights and tinsel, and everyone
gave me presents!

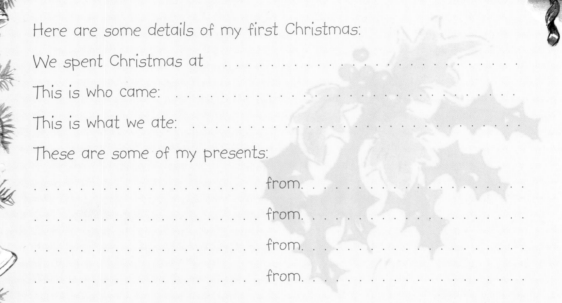

Here are some details of my first Christmas:

We spent Christmas at . . . .

This is who came: . . . .

This is what we ate: . . . .

These are some of my presents:

. . . . from . . . .

. . . . from . . . .

. . . . from . . . .

. . . . from . . . .

The Holly and the Ivy

The holly and the ivy,

When they are both full grown,

Of all the trees that are in the wood,

The holly bears the crown.

My first New Year's celebration was spent at. . . . .
with. . . . .
. . . .
. . . .
. . . .

Christmas Is Coming

Christmas is coming, the geese are getting fat,
Please put a penny in the old man's hat,
If you haven't got a penny, a ha'penny will do,
If you haven't got a ha'penny, God bless you!

 First Vacations

Mommy and Daddy took me on lots of trips and vacations when I was little. I soon discovered what an enormous and interesting world we live in!

We went to . . . . on . . . .

We went with . . . .

We traveled by . . . .

We stayed at . . . .

My favorite activity was . . . .

My favorite outings were . . . .

. . . .

. . . .

. . . .

. . . .

Here is a photograph of me on vacation!

Photo

The World

The world is so full of a number of things
I'm sure we should all be happy as kings!

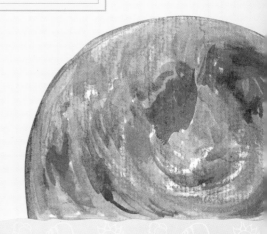

 # My First Birthday

And suddenly I was one year old–didn't time fly! Now I can walk and talk
and do lots of interesting things!

We celebrated my first birthday with (e.g. a party, a special
dinner):

. . . .

I wore:. . . . .

These are the people who helped me celebrate:. . . . .

. . . .

This is what we ate:. . . . .

. . . .

These are some of my presents:

. . . . from. . . . .

. . . . from. . . . .

. . . . from. . . . .

. . . . from. . . . .

And here's a picture of me blowing out the candle on my cake!

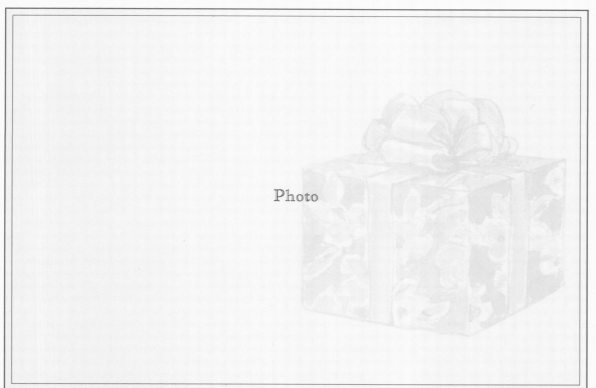

Photo

Favorite Things

It didn't take long to discover which things I liked better than anything else in the world! Here are a few of them.

My favorite nursery rhyme: . . . .

My favorite toys: . . . .

My favorite game: . . . .

My favorite picture: . . . .

My favorite book: . . . .

My favorite people: . . . .

My favorite TV show: . . . .

My favorite animal: . . . .

Things that made me laugh: . . . .

Of course, not everything made me happy! Some of the things I didn't like were . . . .

. . . .

. . . .

The Grand Old Duke of York

Oh, the grand old Duke of York
He had ten thousand men
He marched them up to the top of the hill
And he marched them down again!
And when they were up, they were up
And when they were down, they were down
And when they were only half-way up
They were neither up nor down!

Oranges and Lemons

"Oranges and lemons," say the bells of St. Clements
"You owe me five farthings," say the bells of St. Martins
"When will you pay me?" say the bells of Old Bailey
"When I grow rich," say the bells of Shoreditch
"When will that be?" say the bells of Stepney
"I'm sure I don't know," says the great bell at Bow
Here comes a candle to light you to bed
And here comes a chopper to chop off your head!

Special Memories

My early months are full of special memories.

Visits

My first big visit was a very special occasion that took lots of planning!

Here are some of the details of whom we visited, who came with us,

who was there, what I wore, and how I behaved!

. . . .

. . . .

. . . .

Other memorable visits were:

. . . .

. . . .

. . . .

Baa, Baa, Black Sheep

Baa, baa, black sheep, have you any wool?

Yes sir, yes sir, three bags full

One for the master, one for the dame

And one for the little boy who lives down the lane.

Special moments

Every moment of a baby's life is precious, but here are a few especially
memorable ones that Mommy and Daddy will never forget:

....

....

....

....

The future

Mommy and Daddy have lots of special plans and hopes for my future.

Here are a few of them:

....

....

....

....

I Love Little Pussy

I love little pussy, her coat is so warm

And if I don't hurt her, she'll do me no harm

So I'll not pull her tail, nor drive her away

But pussy and I very gently will play.

Here are some photos of me during my first year:

Photographs